To:

_____

From:

_____

Message:

_____

_____

_____

For God So Loved the World ...

Published by Christian Art Publishers,
PO Box 1599, Vereeniging, 1930, RSA

© 2013
First edition 2013

Designed by Christian Art Publishers

Images used under license from Shutterstock.com

Printed in China

ISBN 978-1-4321-0507-5

For God So Loved the World ...

CHRISTIAN ART
PUBLISHERS

Living, He loved me; dying, He saved me;
Buried, He carried my sins far away;
Rising, He justified freely forever:
One day He's coming — O glorious day!

FROM: ONE DAY

Contents

The Prophecy of a Messiah 9

A Promise Fulfilled 13

Our Savior 15

The Last Supper 19

In the Garden 21

The Road to Calvary 25

The Cross 27

The Empty Tomb 33

Jesus Ascends to Heaven 39

Our Salvation 43

No Greater Love 47

Our Future Hope 53

A Heart of Gratitude 57

An Invitation 61

Living for Jesus 67

Easter always reminds us of the amazing, all-encompassing and unconditional love that God has for us, His children.

It is a time when we remember the sacrifice that Jesus Christ made in order to ensure our salvation and secure our future with Him in heaven. Easter is a time of remembrance, thanksgiving and joy.

Let Easter inspire you to show your gratitude to Christ by spreading the message of His salvation. Show the love of Christ to others by living a life of hope, love and joy.

Let your life be a testimony of the incredible grace of the Father and the selfless sacrifice of the Son.

Happy Easter!

THE PROPHECY
OF A MESSIAH

Praise we the Lord this day,
This day so long foretold,
Whose promise shone with cheering ray
On waiting saints of old.

The prophet gave the sign
For faithful men to read;
A virgin born of David's line
Shall bear the promised seed.

FROM: PRAISE WE THE LORD THIS DAY

Moses continued, "The LORD your God will raise up for you a prophet like me from among your fellow Israelites. You must listen to Him."

DEUT. 18:15

Hail, thou long-expected Jesus,
born to set Thy people free
from our sins and fears release us;
let us find our rest in Thee.

FROM: HAIL, THOU LONG-EXPECTED JESUS

The Lord Himself will give you the sign.
Look! The virgin will conceive a child!
She will give birth to a son and will call
Him Immanuel (which means "God is with us").

ISA. 7:14

Bethlehem and Golgotha, the Manger and the Cross, the birth and the death, must always be seen together.

J. SIDLOW BAXTER

From highest heaven, on joyous wing,
I come to you good news to bring;
Good news I bring, a plenteous store,
Whereof my song shall tell you more.

FROM: FROM HIGHEST HEAVEN, ON JOYOUS WING

"You, Bethlehem Ephrathah, though you are
little among the thousands of Judah, yet out of you
shall come forth to Me the One to be Ruler in Israel,
whose goings forth are from of old, from everlasting."

MIC. 5:2 NKJV

"The time is coming," says the LORD, "when I will
raise up a righteous descendant from King David's line.
He will be a King who rules with wisdom.
He will do what is just and right throughout the land."

JER. 23:5

Rejoice, O people of Zion! Shout in triumph,
O people of Jerusalem! Look, your King is
coming to you. He is righteous and victorious,
yet He is humble, riding on a donkey.

ZECH. 9:9

A PROMISE FULFILLED

O rejoice! O rejoice!
Christ doth come, as long foretold!
The Messiah long expected,
The incarnate Word behold!
Though by kings of earth rejected,
Hail Him Lord of all with mighty voice!
O rejoice! O rejoice!

The hinge of history is on the
door of a Bethlehem stable.

Ralph W. Sockman

Jesus was born in Bethlehem in Judea,
during the reign of King Herod.

Matt. 2:1

Every promise God has ever made
finds its fulfillment in Jesus.

Joni Eareckson Tada

He came to pay a debt He did not owe,
because we owed a debt we could not pay.

Anonymous

Today in the town of David a Savior has been
born to you; He is the Messiah, the Lord.

Luke 2:11 niv

Jesus is the yes to every promise of God.

William Barclay

Our Savior

Man's work faileth, Christ's availeth;
He is all our righteousness;
He, our Savior, has forever
Set us free from dire distress.
Through His merit we inherit
Light and peace and happiness.

FROM: PRAISE THE SAVIOR NOW AND EVER

To us a child is born, to us a son is given,
and the government will be on His shoulders.
And He will be called Wonderful Counselor,
Mighty God, Everlasting Father, Prince of Peace.

Isa. 9:6 niv

In Christ the heart of the Father is revealed,
and higher comfort there cannot be
than to rest in the Father's heart.

Andrew Murray

Jesus is not one of many ways to approach God,
nor is He the best of several ways; He is the only way.

A. W. Tozer

Jesus Christ is the same yesterday, today, and forever.

Heb. 13:8

No man ever loved like Jesus. He taught the blind to see
and the dumb to speak. He died on the cross to save us.
He bore our sins. And now God says,
because He did, I can forgive you.

Billy Graham

In His life, Christ is an example, showing us how to live;
in His death, He is a sacrifice, satisfying our sins;
in His resurrection, a conqueror; in His ascension, a king;
in His intercession, a high priest.

MARTIN LUTHER

The Son is the radiance of God's glory
and the exact representation of His being,
sustaining all things by His powerful word.
After He had provided purification for sins,
He sat down at the right hand of the Majesty in heaven.

HEB. 1:3 NIV

God speaks to me not through the thunder and
the earthquake, nor through the ocean and the stars,
but through the Son of Man, and speaks in a
language adapted to my imperfect sight and hearing.

WILLIAM LYON PHELPS

The Word became human and made His home among us.
He was full of unfailing love and faithfulness.
And we have seen His glory, the glory
of the Father's one and only Son.

JOHN 1:14

THE LAST SUPPER

Bread of the world, in mercy broken,
Wine of the soul, in mercy shed,
By Whom the words of life were spoken,
And in Whose death our sins are dead.

Look on the heart by sorrow broken,
Look on the tears by sinners shed;
And be Thy feast to us the token,
That by Thy grace our souls are fed.

FROM: BREAD OF THE WORLD, IN MERCY BROKEN

As they were eating, Jesus took some bread and
blessed it. Then He broke it in pieces and gave it
to the disciples, saying, "Take this and eat it, for this
is My body." And He took a cup of wine and gave
thanks to God for it. He gave it to them and said,
"Each of you drink from it, for this is My blood, which
confirms the covenant between God and His people.
It is poured out as a sacrifice to forgive the sins of many."

MATT. 26:26-28

The purpose of the Lord's Supper is to
receive from Christ the nourishment and strength
and hope and joy that come from feasting our
souls on all that He purchased for us on
the cross, especially His own fellowship.

JOHN PIPER

The real presence of Christ's most blessed body
and blood is not to be sought for in the sacrament,
but in the worthy receiver of the sacrament.

RICHARD HOOKER

IN THE GARDEN

'Tis midnight and on Olive's brow
the star is dimmed that lately shone;
'Tis midnight in the garden now
the suffering Savior prays alone.

FROM: 'TIS MIDNIGHT AND ON OLIVE'S BROW

Accompanied by the disciples, Jesus left the upstairs
room and went as usual to the Mount of Olives.
There He told them, "Pray that you will not give in to
temptation." He walked away, about a stone's throw,
and knelt down and prayed, "Father, if You are willing,
please take this cup of suffering away from Me. Yet I
want Your will to be done, not Mine." Then an angel
from heaven appeared and strengthened Him. He prayed
more fervently, and He was in such agony of spirit that
His sweat fell to the ground like great drops of blood.
At last He stood up again and returned to the disciples,
only to find them asleep, exhausted from grief.

LUKE 22:39 - 45

Look at Him at Gethsemane, sweating as it were
great drops of blood; look at Him on the cross,
crucified between two thieves; hear that piercing cry,
"Father, Father, forgive them, they know not what
they do." And as you look into that face, as you
look into those wounds on His feet or His hands,
will you say He has not the power to save you?

DWIGHT L. MOODY

Go to dark Gethsemane,
ye that feel the tempter's power;
your Redeemer's conflict see;
watch with Him one bitter hour;
turn not from His griefs away;
learn of Jesus Christ to pray.

FROM: GO TO DARK GETHSEMANE

Even as Jesus said this, a crowd approached,
led by Judas, one of the twelve disciples.
Judas walked over to Jesus to greet Him with a kiss.
But Jesus said, "Judas, would you
betray the Son of Man with a kiss?"

LUKE 22:47-48

23

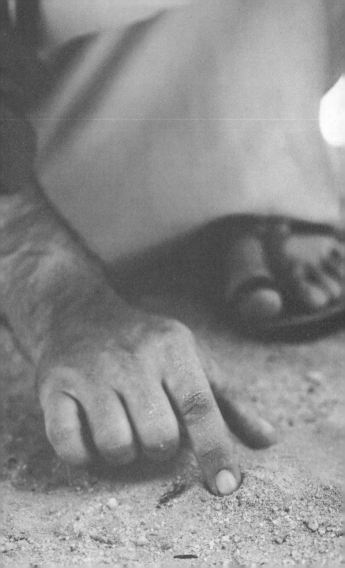

The Road
to Calvary

There is a green hill far away,
Outside a city wall,
Where the dear Lord was crucified,
Who died to save us all.

O dearly, dearly, has He loved,
And we must love Him, too,
And trust in His redeeming blood,
And try His works to do.

From: There Is a Green Hill Far Away

"What crime has He committed?" asked Pilate.
But they shouted all the louder, "Crucify Him!"
Wanting to satisfy the crowd, Pilate released
Barabbas to them. He had Jesus flogged,
and handed Him over to be crucified.

MARK 15:14-15 NIV

He went out, bearing His own cross,
to the place called The Place of a Skull,
which in Aramaic is called Golgotha.

JOHN 19:17 ESV

Up Calvary's mountain one dreadful morn,
walked Christ my Savior weary and worn;
facing for sinners death on the cross
that He might save them from endless loss.

FROM: BLESSED REDEEMER

A passerby named Simon, who was from Cyrene,
was coming in from the countryside just then,
and the soldiers forced him to carry Jesus' cross.

MARK 15:21

THE CROSS

In the cross of Christ I glory,
Towering o'er the wrecks of time;
All the light of sacred story
Gathers round its head sublime.

When the woes of life o'ertake me,
Hopes deceive, and fears annoy,
Never shall the cross forsake me,
Lo! it glows with peace and joy.

FROM: IN THE CROSS OF CHRIST I GLORY

Jesus said, "Father, forgive them,
for they don't know what they are doing."

LUKE 23:34

Jesus replied, "I assure you, today
you will be with Me in paradise."

LUKE 23:43

Jesus shouted, "Father, I entrust
My spirit into Your hands!"

LUKE 23:46

When Jesus saw His mother standing there beside
the disciple He loved, He said to her, "Dear woman,
here is your son." And He said to this disciple,
"Here is your mother." And from then
on this disciple took her into his home.

JOHN 19:26-27

At three o'clock Jesus called out with a loud voice,
"Eloi, Eloi, lema sabachthani?" which means
"My God, My God, why have You abandoned Me?"

MARK 15:34

We believe that the history of the world is but
the history of His influence and that the center
of the whole universe is the cross of Calvary.

ALEXANDER MACLAREN

O Lord Jesus Christ, lifted up upon the
Cross for us that we might see what it is to love;
grant us so to behold and be drawn by Thy love,
that, with all our strength, we may love both
Thee and all for whom Thou didst die.

ANONYMOUS

On a hill far away stood an old rugged cross,
the emblem of suffering and shame;
and I love that old cross where the dearest and best
for a world of sinners was slain.

FROM: THE OLD RUGGED CROSS

There is no man that goeth to heaven but he must
go by the cross. The cross is the standing way-mark
which all they that go to glory must pass by.

JAMES H. AUGHEY

It was about noon, and darkness came over the whole
land until three in the afternoon, for the sun stopped
shining. And the curtain of the temple was torn in two.
Jesus called out with a loud voice,
"Father, into Your hands I commit My spirit."
When He had said this, He breathed His last.
The centurion, seeing what had happened,
praised God and said, "Surely this was a righteous man."

LUKE 23:44-47 NIV

Well might the sun in darkness hide,
and shut his glories in,
when Christ the mighty Maker dies
for man the creature's sin.

FROM: ALAS, AND DID MY SAVIOR BLEED

O Christ, give us patience and faith and hope, as we
kneel at the foot of Thy cross, and hold fast to it.
Teach us by Thy cross that however ill the world may go,
the Father so loved us that He spared not Thee.

CHARLES KINGSLEY

When Christ was hung on the cross,
He took upon Himself the curse for our wrongdoing.

GAL. 3:13

Mercy there was great, and grace was free;
pardon there was multiplied to me;
there my burdened soul found liberty at Calvary.

From: At Calvary

The cross is the lightning rod of grace that
short-circuits God's wrath to Christ so that
only the light of His love remains for believers.

A. W. Tozer

At the cross there's room!
Streams of boundless mercy flow,
free to all who thither go;
oh, that all the world might know
at the cross there's room!

From: At the Cross There's Room

The greatest adventure in life — knowing God — begins
at the cross of Christ and ends with a "Hallelujah!"

David Jeremiah

THE EMPTY TOMB

Joy dawned again on Easter Day,
The sun shone out with fairer ray,
When, to their longing eyes restored
Th' Apostles saw their risen Lord.

FROM: JOY DAWNED AGAIN ON EASTER DAY

He is not here, for He has risen, as He said.
Come, see the place where He lay.

MATT. 28:6 ESV

"I am the resurrection and the life. Anyone who
believes in Me will live, even after dying. Everyone
who lives in Me and believes in Me will never ever die."

JOHN 11:25-26

Up from the grave He arose,
with a mighty triumph over His foes;
He arose a victor from the dark domain,
and He lives forever with His saints to reign.
He arose! He arose! Hallelujah Christ arose!

FROM: LOW IN THE GRAVE HE LAY

Our Lord has written the promise of the resurrection
not in books alone, but in every leaf in springtime.

MARTIN LUTHER

Tomb, thou shalt not hold Him longer;
Death is strong, but Life is stronger;
Stronger than the dark, the light;
Stronger than the wrong, the right;
Faith and Hope triumphant say
Christ will rise on Easter Day.

PHILLIPS BROOKS

Christ died for our sins, just as the Scriptures said.
He was buried, and He was raised from the dead
on the third day, just as the Scriptures said.

1 COR. 15:3-4

Jesus Christ is risen today,
Our triumphant holy day;
Who did once upon the cross
Suffer to redeem our loss.
Hallelujah!

FROM: JESUS CHRIST IS RISEN TODAY

Our old history ends with the cross;
our new history begins with the resurrection.

WATCHMAN NEE

Where, O death, is your victory?
Where, O death, is your sting?

1 COR. 15:55 NIV

Blessed be the God and Father of our Lord Jesus Christ!
According to His great mercy, He has caused us
to be born again to a living hope through the
resurrection of Jesus Christ from the dead.

1 PET. 1:3 ESV

The stone was rolled away from the door, not to permit
Christ to come out, but to enable the disciples to go in.

PETER MARSHALL

Easter says you can put truth in a grave,
but it won't stay there.

CLARENCE W. HALL

Although we have complete salvation through His death,
because we are reconciled to God by it,
it is by His resurrection, not His death,
that we are said to be born to a living hope.

JOHN CALVIN

We live and die; Christ died and lived!

JOHN STOTT

The resurrection gives my life meaning
and direction and the opportunity to start
over no matter what my circumstances.

ROBERT FLATT

Lives again our glorious King, Alleluia!
Where, O death, is now thy sting? Alleluia!
Once He died our souls to save, Alleluia!
Where's thy victory, boasting grave? Alleluia!

FROM: CHRIST THE LORD IS RISEN

Jesus Ascends to Heaven

O risen Christ, ascended Lord,
All praise to Thee let earth accord,
Who art, while endless ages run,
With Father and with Spirit One.

FROM: SING WE TRIUMPHANT HYMNS OF PRAISE

Then the eleven disciples went to Galilee,
to the mountain where Jesus had told them to go.
When they saw Him, they worshiped Him;
but some doubted. Then Jesus came to them and said,
"All authority in heaven and on earth has been given
to Me. Therefore go and make disciples of all nations,
baptizing them in the name of the Father and of the
Son and of the Holy Spirit, and teaching them to
obey everything I have commanded you. And surely
I am with you always, to the very end of the age."

MATT. 28:16-20 NIV

When we've been there ten thousand years,
bright shining as the sun,
we've no less days to sing God's praise
than when we'd first begun.

FROM: AMAZING GRACE

"If I go and prepare a place for you,
I will come back and take you to be
with Me that you also may be where I am."

JOHN 14:3 NIV

He led them out as far as Bethany, and He lifted
up His hands and blessed them. Now it came to pass,
while He blessed them, that He was parted from them
and carried up into heaven. And they worshiped Him,
and returned to Jerusalem with great joy, and were
continually in the temple praising and blessing God.

LUKE 24:50-53 NKJV

When the heavens shall ring,
and the angels sing, at Thy coming to victory,
let Thy voice call me home, saying, "Yet there is room,
there is room at My side for thee."

FROM: THOU DIDST LEAVE THY THRONE

He departed from our sight that we
might return to our heart, and there find Him.
For He departed, and behold, He is here.

ST. AUGUSTINE

Before the Resurrection of Christ, the Holy Spirit came
upon individuals only on certain occasions for special
tasks. But now, after the Resurrection, Christ through
the Holy Spirit dwells in the heart of every believer to
give us supernatural power in living our daily lives.

BILLY GRAHAM

When the Day of Pentecost arrived, they were all
together in one place. And suddenly there came from
heaven a sound like a mighty rushing wind, and it
filled the entire house where they were sitting.
And divided tongues as of fire appeared
to them and rested on each one of them.
And they were all filled with the Holy Spirit.

ACTS 2:1- 4 ESV

O Holy Ghost, giver of light and life;
impart to us thoughts higher than our own thoughts,
and prayers better than our own prayers,
and powers beyond our own powers;
that we may spend and be spent
in the ways of love and goodness,
after the perfect image of
our Lord and Savior Jesus Christ.

E. MILNER- WHITE

OUR SALVATION

I must needs go home by the way of the cross,
There's no other way but this;
I shall ne'er get sight of the gates of light,
If the way of the cross I miss.

The way of the cross leads home,
The way of the cross leads home,
It is sweet to know as I onward go,
The way of the cross leads home.

FROM: THE WAY OF THE CROSS LEADS HOME

The cross is God's truth about us, and therefore it
is the only power which can make us truthful. When
we know the cross we are no longer afraid of the truth.

DIETRICH BONHOEFFER

Easter spells out beauty, the rare beauty of new life.

S. D. GORDON

He was wounded for our transgressions, He was bruised
for our iniquities; the chastisement for our peace
was upon Him, and by His stripes we are healed.

ISA. 53:5 NKJV

Rock of Ages, cleft for me,
Let me hide myself in Thee;
Let the water and the blood,
From Thy wounded side which flowed,
Be of sin the double cure,
Save from wrath and make me pure.

FROM: ROCK OF AGES

Salvation is free for you because someone else paid.

ANONYMOUS

In the cross of Christ I see three things:
First, a description of the depth of man's sin.
Second, the overwhelming love of God.
Third, the only way of salvation.

BILLY GRAHAM

"I am the way, the truth, and the life.
No one can come to the Father except through Me."

JOHN 14:6

Calvary not merely made possible the salvation of those
for whom Christ died; it ensured that they would be
brought to faith and their salvation made actual.

J. I. PACKER

Believe in the Lord Jesus and you will be saved.

ACTS 16:31

"I am the gate. Those who come in through
Me will be saved. They will come and go
freely and will find good pastures."

JOHN 10:9

God takes care of His own. He knows our needs.
He anticipates our crises. He is moved by our
weaknesses. He stands ready to come to our rescue.
And at just the right moment He steps in and
proves Himself as our faithful heavenly Father.

CHARLES SWINDOLL

Today Jesus Christ is being dispatched as the
Figurehead of a Religion, a mere example.
He is that, but He is infinitely more;
He is salvation itself, He is the Gospel of God.

OSWALD CHAMBERS

I trust in Your unfailing love;
my heart rejoices in Your salvation.

PS. 13:5 NIV

Salvation is not something that is done
for you but something that happens within you.
It is not the clearing of a court record,
but the transformation of a life attitude.

ALBERT W. PALMER

No Greater Love

God loved the world so tenderly
His only Son He gave,
That all who on His Name believe
Its wondrous power will save.

For God so loved the world
that He gave His only Son,
That whosoever believeth in Him
Should not perish, should not perish;
That whosoever believeth in Him
Should not perish, but have everlasting life.

From: God So Loved the World

Since He did not spare even His own Son
but gave Him up for us all,
won't He also give us everything else?

ROM. 8:32

God proved His love on the cross.
When Christ hung, and bled, and died
it was God saying to the world — I love you.

BILLY GRAHAM

I love Thee because Thou has first loved me,
and purchased my pardon on Calvary's tree.
I love Thee for wearing the thorns on Thy brow;
If ever I loved Thee, my Jesus, 'tis now.

FROM: JESUS, I LOVE THEE

Greater love has no one than this:
to lay down one's life for one's friends.

JOHN 15:13 NIV

Because of His great love for us, God, who is rich
in mercy, made us alive with Christ even when we
were dead in transgressions — it is by grace you
have been saved. And God raised us up with Christ
and seated us with Him in the heavenly realms
in Christ Jesus, in order that in the coming ages
He might show the incomparable riches of His grace,
expressed in His kindness to us in Christ Jesus.
For it is by grace you have been saved, through faith —
and this is not from yourselves, it is the gift of God —
not by works, so that no one can boast.

EPH. 2:4 - 9 NIV

"God so loved the world, that He gave His only Son,
that whoever believes in Him should
not perish but have eternal life."

JOHN 3:16 ESV

By the cross we know the gravity of sin
and the greatness of God's love towards us.

JOHN CHRYSOSTOM

Being found in appearance as a man,
He humbled Himself and became obedient
to the point of death, even the death of the cross.

PHIL. 2:8 NKJV

God demonstrates His own love for us in this:
While we were still sinners, Christ died for us.

ROM. 5:8 NIV

In all these things we are more than conquerors through
Him who loved us. I am convinced that neither death
nor life, neither angels nor demons, neither the present
nor the future, nor any powers, neither height nor depth,
nor anything else in all creation, will be able to separate
us from the love of God that is in Christ Jesus our Lord.

ROM. 8:37-39 NIV

Very rarely will anyone die for a righteous person, though for a good person someone might possibly dare to die. But God demonstrates His own love for us in this: While we were still sinners, Christ died for us. Since we have now been justified by His blood, how much more shall we be saved from God's wrath through Him! For if, while we were God's enemies, we were reconciled to Him through the death of His Son, how much more, having been reconciled, shall we be saved through His life! Not only is this so, but we also boast in God through our Lord Jesus Christ, through whom we have now received reconciliation.

Rom. 5:7-11 niv

OUR FUTURE HOPE

———✦———

Christ, our loving Mediator,
Now with God for you and me
Intercedes, and our Creator
Hears and answers every plea.

Hail Him! Hail Him!
Tell the story!
Hail! all hail!
Jesus lives forevermore.

FROM: CHRIST, WHO LEFT HIS HOME IN GLORY

He is a portion that exactly, and directly suits —
the condition of the soul,
the desires of the soul,
the necessities of the soul,
the wants of the soul,
the longings of the soul,
and the prayers of the soul.
The soul can crave nothing,
nor wish for nothing,
but what is to be found in Christ.
He is light to enlighten the soul,
wisdom to counsel the soul,
power to support the soul,
goodness to supply the soul,
mercy to pardon the soul,
beauty to delight the soul,
glory to ravish the soul,
and fullness to fill the soul.

THOMAS BROOKS

We are citizens of heaven, where the Lord Jesus Christ
lives. And we are eagerly waiting for Him to
return as our Savior. He will take our weak
mortal bodies and change them into glorious
bodies like His own, using the same power with
which He will bring everything under His control.

PHIL. 3:20-21

To Him be Glory and Power, now and forever,
and from all ages to all ages. Amen!

JOHN CHRYSOSTOM

Heaven will be the perfection we have always longed for.
All the things that made Earth unlovely
and tragic will be absent in Heaven.

BILLY GRAHAM

There are better things ahead than any we leave behind.

C. S. LEWIS

Heaven is a prepared place for prepared people.

LEWIS SPERRY CHAFER

A Heart of
Gratitude

I will sing the wondrous story
of the Christ Who died for me.
How He left His home in glory
for the cross of Calvary.

Yes, I'll sing the wondrous story
of the Christ Who died for me,
sing it with the saints in glory,
gathered by the crystal sea.

I was lost, but Jesus found me,
found the sheep that went astray,
threw His loving arms around me,
drew me back into His way.

From: I Will Sing the Wondrous Story

Spring bursts today, for Christ is
risen and all the earth's at play.

CHRISTINA ROSSETTI

Thank God for this gift too wonderful for words!

2 COR. 9:15

Thanks be to You, my Lord Jesus Christ,
for all the benefits You have won for me.
For all the pains and insults
You have borne for me.
O most merciful Redeemer, Friend, and Brother,
may I know You more clearly,
love You more dearly,
and follow You more nearly,
day by day.

RICHARD OF CHICHESTER

Man of Sorrows! What a name
For the Son of God, who came
Ruined sinners to reclaim!
Hallelujah, what a Savior!

PHILIP P. BLISS

What a wonderful change in my life has been wrought
Since Jesus came into my heart!
I have light in my soul for which long I had sought,
Since Jesus came into my heart!

FROM: SINCE JESUS CAME INTO MY HEART

Jesus is moved to happiness every time He sees that
you appreciate what He has done for you. Grip His
pierced hand and say to Him, "I thank Thee, Savior,
because Thou hast died for me."

O. HALLESBY

We welcome glad Easter when Jesus arose,
and won a great victory over His foes.
Then raise your glad voices, all Christians and sing,
Bring glad Easter tidings to Jesus, your King.

FROM: WE WELCOME GLAD EASTER

Let us run
with *endurance*
the race that is
set before us,
looking to Jesus,
the
founder
and *perfecter*
of our faith,
who for the
joy that was set
before Him
endured the cross,
and is seated at the right
hand of the
throne of *God.*

HEB. 12:1-2 ESV

An Invitation

What the invitation is about:

- *Accepting Jesus as your Lord and Savior*
- *Believing with your heart that Jesus lived,*
  died and rose again
- *Believing that there is no other*
  way to heaven but through Jesus
- *Asking God to create a new heart and spirit in you*
- *Trusting and finding rest in Him alone.*

All have sinned and fall short of the glory of God.

ROM. 3:23 NKJV

Hungry for love, He looks at you. Thirsty for kindness,
He begs of you. Naked for loyalty, He hopes in you.
Homeless for shelter in your heart, He asks of you.
Will you be that one to Him?

MOTHER TERESA

No man is excluded from calling upon God,
the gate of salvation is set open unto all men:
neither is there any other thing which keepeth us
back from entering in, save only our own unbelief.

JOHN CALVIN

"Anyone who believes in God's Son has eternal life.
Anyone who doesn't obey the Son will never experience
eternal life but remains under God's angry judgment."

JOHN 3:36

There is, however, equally great incentive to
worship and love God in the thought that,
for some unfathomable reason, He wants me as
His friend, and desires to be my friend, and has given
His Son to die for me in order to realize this purpose.
Not merely that we know God, but that He knows us.

J. I. PACKER

Because God has made us for Himself,
our hearts are restless until they rest in Him.

ST. AUGUSTINE

The Lord is not slow in keeping His promise,
as some understand slowness. Instead He is
patient with you, not wanting anyone to perish,
but everyone to come to repentance.

2 PET. 3.9 NIV

But when you take the Bible literally, for what it says,
you have to come back to the fact that there is only
one way of salvation; there's only one Savior.

TIM LaHAYE

63

For by grace you have been saved through faith.
And this is not your own doing; it is the gift of God.

Eph. 2:8 esv

I came all this way for a reason.
Today is the day of salvation. Trust Jesus to save you.
Then be sincere as God knows a pretender.

Kirk Cameron

When God our Savior revealed His kindness and love,
He saved us, not because of the righteous things
we had done, but because of His mercy. He washed
away our sins, giving us a new birth and new life through
the Holy Spirit. He generously poured out the Spirit
upon us through Jesus Christ our Savior. Because of
His grace He declared us righteous and gave us
confidence that we will inherit eternal life.

Titus 3:4-7

Through salvation our past has been forgiven,
our present is given meaning, and our future is secured.

Rick Warren

Salvation is found in no one else,
for there is no other name under heaven
given to mankind by which we must be saved.

ACTS 4:12 NIV

My salvation was a free gift. I didn't have to work for it
and it's better than any gold medal that I've ever won.

BETTY CUTHBERT

Beloved, now we are children of God; and it has
not yet been revealed what we shall be, but we know
that when He is revealed, we shall be like Him,
for we shall see Him as He is.

1 JOHN 3:2 NKJV

If you confess with your mouth that
Jesus is Lord and believe in your heart that
God raised Him from the dead, you will be saved.
For with the heart one believes and is justified,
and with the mouth one confesses and is saved.

ROM. 10:9-10 ESV

Let me address all of you, high and low, rich and poor,
one with another, to accept of mercy and grace
while it is offered to you; now is the accepted time,
now is the day of salvation; and will you not accept it,
now it is offered unto you?

GEORGE WHITEFIELD

Is today the first time you have seriously considered
the preceding verses and quotes and would like
to accept Jesus as your Lord and Savior?
Don't put it off until tomorrow — today is the day!
Jesus died for you two thousand years ago;
if you had been the only person on earth, He would
have still done so! Isn't that amazing? If you have never
come to salvation, you can receive eternal life right now
by believing in Jesus. He is waiting with open arms.

LIVING FOR JESUS

Nearer, my God, to Thee, nearer to Thee!
E'en though it be a cross that raiseth me,
still all my song shall be, nearer, my God, to Thee.
Nearer, my God, to Thee,
Nearer to Thee!

FROM: NEARER, MY GOD, TO THEE

Those who say they live in God
should live their lives as Jesus did.

1 John 2:6

Fix your thoughts on what is true, and honorable,
and right, and pure, and lovely, and admirable. Think
about things that are excellent and worthy of praise.

Phil. 4:8

Trust in the LORD and do good.
Then you will live safely in the land and prosper.
Take delight in the LORD, and He will give you
your heart's desires. Commit everything you do to
the LORD. Trust Him, and He will help you.

Ps. 37:3-5

More like Jesus would I be, let my Savior dwell with me;
fill my soul with peace and love —
make me gentle as a dove;
more like Jesus, while I go, pilgrim in this world below;
poor in spirit would I be; let my Savior dwell in me.

FROM: MORE LIKE JESUS WOULD I BE